Science Detective

Jane Glover
Advisory Teacher for Language and Reading Development, Cambridgeshire

David Glover
Formerly Lecturer in Science, Cambridgeshire College of Arts and Technology

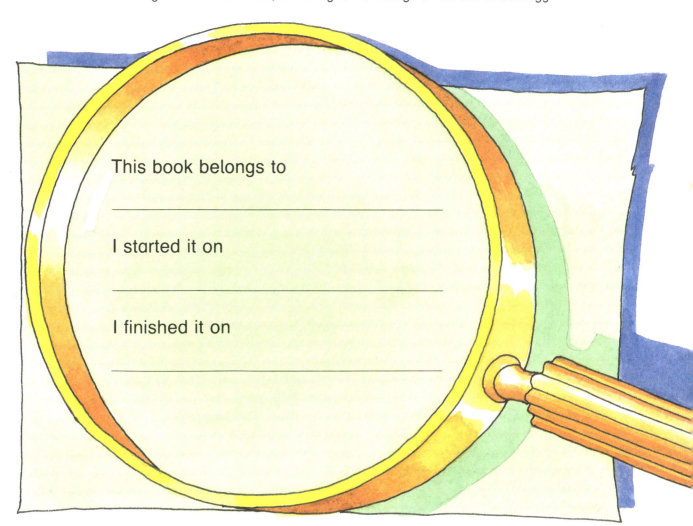

This book belongs to

_____

I started it on

_____

I finished it on

_____

Illustrated by Graham Round

1

To Parents

In today's world children grow up surrounded by the products of science and technology. With the introduction of the National Curriculum, science is now a central part of study in all schools. From the first year in the infant school, science activities are introduced to help develop observation and problem solving skills, as well as to stimulate children's curiosity about the world around them.

This series of books is specially designed to develop children's scientific knowledge and skills through activities that are fun and easy to do at home with everyday materials. The activities follow closely the approach to science adopted in the National Curriculum. Working through them will give your child a sound basis for achieving his or her full potential in science at school.

Trying out science experiments at home will help build your child's confidence and enthusiasm for science at school. In this respect girls are sometimes at a disadvantage when compared with boys – they may lack confidence in their abilities in science simply because they have not been given the same opportunities to play with construction kits or technical toys at home. We hope that both girls and boys will enjoy the activities in this book and discover the fun of science.

Working together can be a very rewarding experience for parents as well as children. This book provides lots of opportunities to share in your child's learning and to show that you value your child's ideas and discoveries.

How to use this book

Check the introduction and notes to the chosen activity and make sure that you have all the materials you will need.

Read the instructions with your child and talk about the activity. Make sure that your child understands what to do.

Join in the activity – but try to let your child take the lead. Encourage your child to try things out and ask questions rather than immediately showing the child what to do.

Don't try to do too much at one time; one activity a session is probably enough for a child of 6+.

Talk about the activity at every stage. Encourage your child to discuss observations and discoveries as they are made.

There are **notes** throughout the book to help you. On page 32 you will find a more detailed explanation of the ways in which the activities help to develop children's scientific thinking and knowledge and link to the National Curriculum.

There is a pull-out **games board** in the centre of this book. Games are of value in learning because they enable children to practise skills or memorise facts in an enjoyable way.

These activities have already been tried out and enjoyed by many children in the classroom. We hope that you and your child will enjoy discovering science with them at home!

Jane & David Glover

Science detectives!

In this book the science gang are having fun looking for clues and doing lots more experiments.

Water fun

Can you make a needle float?

You will need

a needle
a bowl full of water
a paper clip
some soap or
washing up liquid

Note to Parents
Both these experiments rely on
surface tension. This gives the
water surface some strength
like a delicate skin. The needle
is not heavy enough to break
through the water surface. Soap
reduces surface tension so the
needle sinks. (Make sure your
child knows what polluted
means.)

In the second experiment, the
surface tension of the water
between the rim of the glass and
the card stops the air getting in,
so the water can't get out. Air
pressure from the outside holds
the card in place.

What to do

Bend the paper clip like this.

Rest the needle on the paper clip.

Lower the needle on the paper clip very gently into the water. You
can rest your wrist on the side of the bowl to steady your hand.
Remove the paper clip very carefully – without touching the needle.

The needle is resting on the water
surface. The surface is like a skin!

You may have to try several times before you manage to make
the needle float!

Make your fingertips soapy. Touch the water near the needle.
What happens?

Have you seen insects walking on the water
in streams and ponds? They rest on the
surface of the water just like the needle did.

Why is it bad for insects if streams and ponds
are polluted with soapy water?

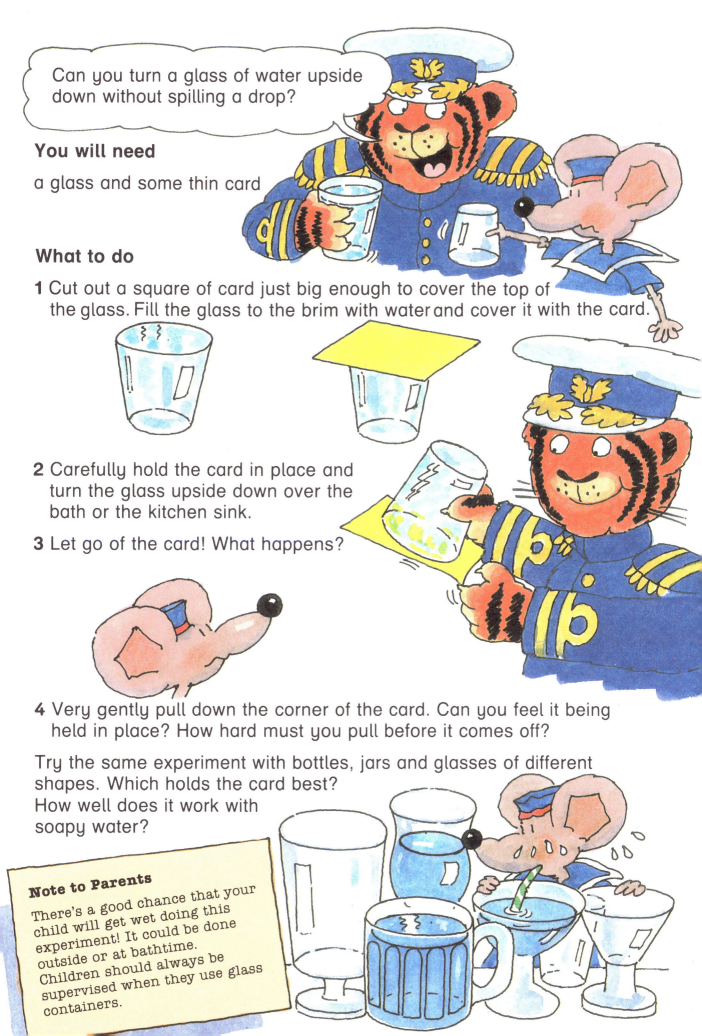

Can you turn a glass of water upside down without spilling a drop?

You will need

a glass and some thin card

What to do

1 Cut out a square of card just big enough to cover the top of the glass. Fill the glass to the brim with water and cover it with the card.

2 Carefully hold the card in place and turn the glass upside down over the bath or the kitchen sink.

3 Let go of the card! What happens?

4 Very gently pull down the corner of the card. Can you feel it being held in place? How hard must you pull before it comes off?

Try the same experiment with bottles, jars and glasses of different shapes. Which holds the card best?
How well does it work with soapy water?

Note to Parents
There's a good chance that your child will get wet doing this experiment! It could be done outside or at bathtime. Children should always be supervised when they use glass containers.

Teeth

Different animals have different kinds of teeth.

Rabbits have sharp front teeth for nibbling roots and cutting leaves and grass.

Dogs have pointed front teeth for tearing meat and strong side teeth for crunching bones.

What sorts of teeth have you got? You will need an apple and a mirror to find out.

Bite a piece of the apple. Did you use your front teeth or your side teeth? Tick the right box.

biting teeth   front ☐

side ☐

Now chew the piece of apple. Which teeth did you use this time?
Tick the right box.

chewing teeth   front ☐

side ☐

Use a mirror to help you fill in this chart.

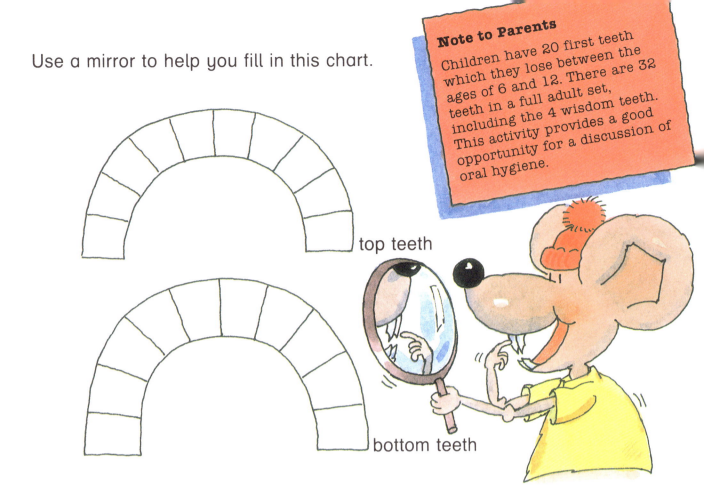

Note to Parents

Children have 20 first teeth which they lose between the ages of 6 and 12. There are 32 teeth in a full adult set, including the 4 wisdom teeth. This activity provides a good opportunity for a discussion of oral hygiene.

top teeth

bottom teeth

Colour your sharp biting teeth red. Colour your broad chewing teeth blue. If you have any missing teeth leave the square blank. Mark teeth that have a filling with a cross, x.

How many teeth have you got altogether?

Try to find a grown up who will let you count his or her teeth. Make a chart like the one above showing how many teeth he or she has.

Whose teeth are these?

Think about the food that mice, tigers and crocodiles eat. Draw lines to join Mix, Tiger and Cruncher to their teeth.

Cotton reel engines

This is how you can make a cotton reel engine.

You will need

a cotton reel
a used matchstick
a short strong rubber band (about the length of a cotton reel)
a pencil
a washer or a small nut
sticky tape

What to do

Thread the rubber band through the cotton reel.

Break the matchstick in half. Put one half of it through one end of the rubber band.

Pull the other end of the rubber band through the washer. Push the pencil through the loop that is left.

Stick the half matchstick to the cotton reel with some sticky tape.

rubber band

washer

matchstick

pencil

Your cotton reel engine is ready to go!

Note to Parents

If you do not have a small brass or steel washer, cut a slice off the end of a small candle. Bore a hole through it with a skewer to make an effective washer.

It is difficult to get this engine to work if the rubber band is too long. If it doesn't work the first time, try a shorter or thicker elastic band.

8

Hold the reel in one hand. Turn the pencil to wind up the band with the other hand. Wind until the band is tight.

Note to Parents
All engines need a source of energy to make them go. In this engine, energy is stored in the rubber band when it is wound up.

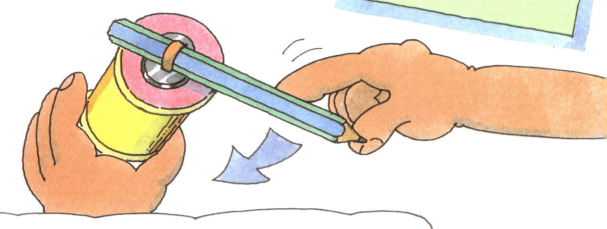

Let the engine go on the floor. It should whizz off!

Some experiments to try

1 Count 15 turns as you wind the engine up. How far does it go?

2 How far does it go with 30 turns?

3 Which surface does it go best on – carpet, tiles, concrete or grass?

4 Make a slope with some books and card. Will your engine climb the slope? How steep a slope can it climb?

5 Will your engine pull a load?

Plants and water

I keep watering these flowers.

What happens to all the water?

Note to Parents

Experiment 1 shows that plants take up water. There is some water loss by evaporation from the top of each vase, but most of the water disappears because it is taken up by the twigs.

Experiment 2 shows that plants give off some of the water they take up.

Try these experiments to find out about plants and water.

Experiment 1

You will need some leafy twigs
two narrow glass vases or bottles

What to do

Put the twigs in one vase.

Fill both vases to the top with water.

Leave them for 24 hours on a window sill.

In which vase does the water level drop most? Tick the right box.

The one with twigs ☐   The one without twigs ☐

Experiment 2

You will need a polythene bag
an elastic band

What to do

Put the polythene bag over the twigs in the vase. Close it with the elastic band. Leave it overnight. What happens to the inside of the bag?

It _____

A garden that doesn't need watering!

This is a bottle garden. You can plant your own in an old sweet jar or a large coffee jar with a screw lid. Ask a grown up to help you.

You will need

a large glass jar with a lid
potting compost
some small stones
some plants to grow – small, well-established plants that like a warm, damp atmosphere are best. Try ferns, miniature ivy, African violets, mosses, begonias, spider plants.

What to do

Cover the bottom of the jar with a layer of small stones. Cover the stones with potting compost to a depth of about 8 cm (3 inches).

Sprinkle the compost with water.

Use an old spoon or fork tied to a stick to help you put your plants in the jar. 3 or 4 plants are enough.

The plants' roots take up water from the soil and it comes out through the leaves, just like you saw in Experiment 2 on the opposite page. The water can't escape from the bottle – it goes back into the soil and the garden doesn't need watering. If your jar steams up, take the lid off for an hour or two to let it clear.

Static electricity

Note to Parents

These experiments work best on a warm, dry day. On a damp day the results will be disappointin[g]

Explain that attract means pull together and repel means push apart.

You will need

2 balloons
a woollen cloth or an old wool sweater

What to do

Blow up the balloons.

Rub one of the balloons with the cloth or sweater. This will charge it with **static electricity.**

Rub the balloon 5 or 6 times in one direction…
you can tell when it's charged because it will stick to the wall…

Try these experiments with a charged balloon.

Make your friend's hair stand on end! Slowly bring a charged balloon up to your friend's hair. Watch what happens!

Tear up some paper into tiny pieces. Hold a charged balloon near them. What happens?

Do the same experiment with other small objects. Try grains of rice, polystyrene, paper clips and used matchsticks. Which ones does the balloon attract?

Hold a charged balloon near a stream of water running from a tap. Is the water attracted or repelled? Tick the right box.

attracted ☐

repelled ☐

Ask a helper to hold a charged balloon by the tied end. Charge your other balloon. Bring it slowly towards the first balloon. Is your balloon attracted or repelled? Tick the right box.

attracted ☐

repelled ☐

Soil

Soil is full of living things. How many can you find?

You will need

a trowel
a small bucket – you could use the one you take to the beach
some sheets of newspaper
yoghurt pots
an old spoon
an old paint brush

What to do

Fill your bucket with soil.

Spread out the newspaper and tip your soil on to it. What can you find?

Use your spoon and paint brush to sort what's there.

You could sort all the different things into yoghurt pots.

Don't handle the animals with your fingers – you may hurt them!

Use the chart on the next page to make lists of all the living and non-living things that you find. Count how many of each sort there are and put the number next to the name on the list.

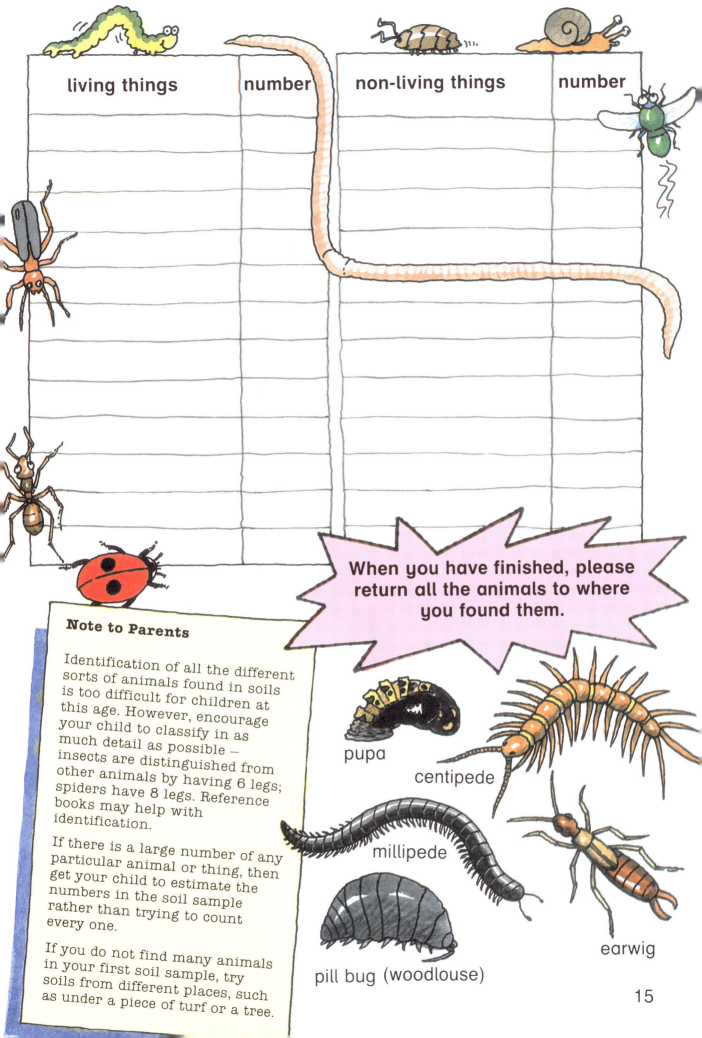

living things	number	non-living things	number

When you have finished, please return all the animals to where you found them.

pupa

centipede

millipede

pill bug (woodlouse)

earwig

Note to Parents

Identification of all the different sorts of animals found in soils is too difficult for children at this age. However, encourage your child to classify in as much detail as possible — insects are distinguished from other animals by having 6 legs; spiders have 8 legs. Reference books may help with identification.

If there is a large number of any particular animal or thing, then get your child to estimate the numbers in the soil sample rather than trying to count every one.

If you do not find many animals in your first soil sample, try soils from different places, such as under a piece of turf or a tree.

Fingerprints

Everybody's fingerprints are different. Here are some common shapes.

whorl   arch   loop   composite

Can you take your own fingerprints?

You will need

a thick felt-tipped pen and some paper

What to do

1 Ink your fingertip with the pen. Work quickly so that the ink on the doesn't dry.

2 Press your finger on to some paper. Roll it from side to side to make a print.

3 Practise until you can make good clean prints.

4 Fill in your fingerprint chart on the next page.

Note to Parents

An ink pad is better for inking the fingers than a felt tip, if you have one. Margarine can be substituted for petroleum jelly.

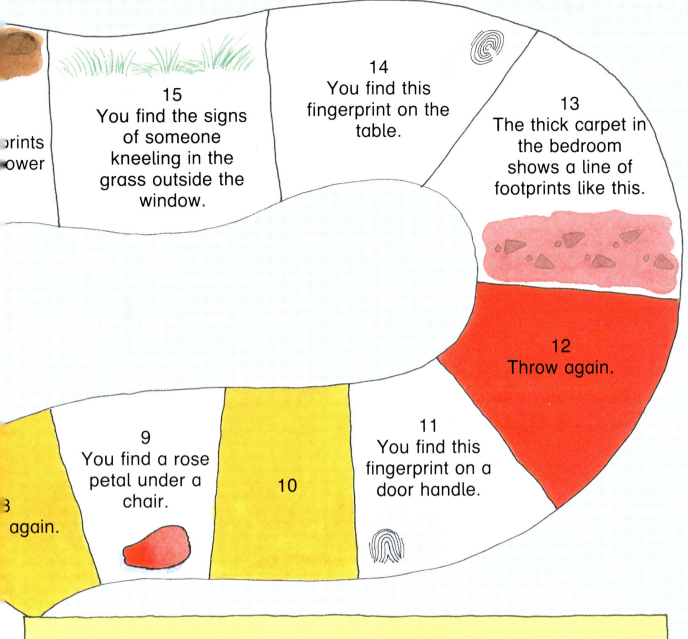

15
You find the signs of someone kneeling in the grass outside the window.

14
You find this fingerprint on the table.

13
The thick carpet in the bedroom shows a line of footprints like this.

12
Throw again.

11
You find this fingerprint on a door handle.

9
You find a rose petal under a chair.

10

rints
ower

3
again.

The Case

There has been a robbery at Inglenook Mansion. There are 3 likely suspects and you are one of the detectives investigating the crime.

To play the game

You need someone to play with, 2 buttons or counters, 12 used matchsticks and a dice.

Choose one suspect each from the 3 pictures at the top of the board. Put a match on each clue on the trail. Take it in turn to throw the dice and move around the scene of the crime. Every time you reach a clue connecting your suspect with the crime pick up the match on that square. The first player to collect 3 clues connecting his or her suspect with the crime is the winner. You may have to go round the board more than once.

Space game

You will need

someone to play with
8 red counters (or pieces of card or paper)
8 blue counters (or pieces of card or paper)
a dice
2 buttons

1 Mercury

2 Venus

3 Earth

4 Mars

J

Sun

How to play

Put the 2 buttons on planet Earth.

Put a red counter and a blue counter on each of the other planets – remember the Sun is a **star** not a planet.

Choose your button and the colour of your counters. Take it in turn to throw the dice. Move from planet to planet away from or towards the Sun. Change direction when you pass Pluto or Mercury. For example, if you throw a five, you can either go away from the Sun to Neptune or towards the Sun to Mercury, change direction and land on Mars.

When you first land on a planet, collect your counter. The first person to have visited all the planets and landed back on Earth is the winner.

9

8   Pluto

Neptune

7

Uranus

6

Saturn

r

Detective trail

The suspects

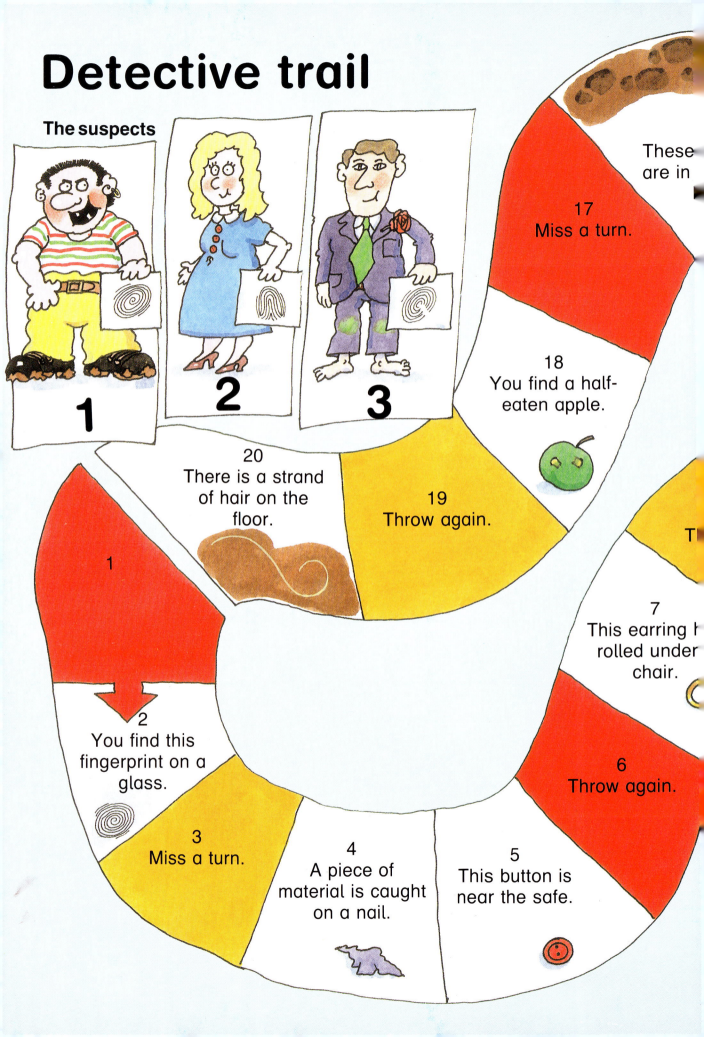

1

2

3

These are in

17
Miss a turn.

18
You find a half-eaten apple.

20
There is a strand of hair on the floor.

19
Throw again.

T

7
This earring rolled under chair.

1

2
You find this fingerprint on a glass.

6
Throw again.

3
Miss a turn.

4
A piece of material is caught on a nail.

5
This button is near the safe.

Fingerprint record

left hand

little finger

Name_____

Date _____

thumb

right hand

thumb

little finger

Write **whorl, arch, loop** or **composite** under each print.

Fingerprint detectives

You will need

a clean glass
some petroleum jelly
2 or 3 people to play with

What to do

A magnifying glass will help you.

1 Take the fingerprints from the thumb and first finger of each person.

2 Decide who is the detective. The detective should leave the room.

3 One person makes their fingers greasy with a little petroleum jelly and picks up the glass.

4 Ask the detective to come back into the room.

5 Who held the glass? Can the detective decide by matching the fingerprints on the glass to one person's fingerprints?

6 Now someone else can be the detective.

17

Colours

Mixing colours

You will need

6 felt-tipped pens with these colours.

What to do

Colour the white circle with one of the colours.

Before it is dry, colour it over with the other colour.
What colour is the mixture?

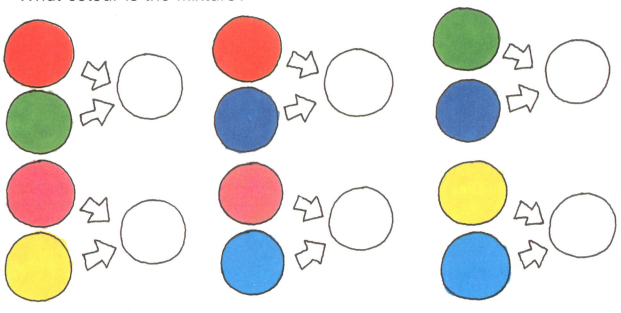

Which pairs give bright colours? Try your own combinations on a separate sheet of paper.

Note to Parents

With **light**, mixing pairs of the **primary** colours (red, green and blue) produces the **secondary** colours (magenta, yellow and cyan – as above). With paints it is different. Mixing pairs of red, green and blue produces a dark brown or black. Mixing magenta, yellow and cyan produces bright colours.

Separating colours

Coloured inks, paints and dies are often made by mixing different colours together. This is how you can separate the mixture.

You will need

Some strips of blotting paper 25 cm long by 1 cm wide (10 inches by ½ inch), 2 bottles, a dish of clean water, some clothes pegs, string, some colours to test – try felt-tip ink, food colouring, blackcurrant juice, for example.

What to do

1 Tie the string about 20 cm (8 inches) above the water. You could tie it between 2 bottles.

2 Put a line of the colour you are testing 5 cm (2 inches) from one end of the blotting paper strip.

3 Peg the strip on the string so that the end with the coloured line is about 1 cm (½ inch) in the water.

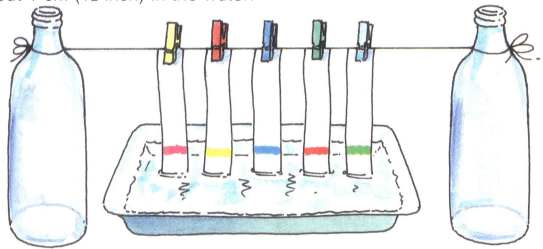

4 Watch how the colour is separated as the water soaks along the blotting paper.

Police scientists do experiments like this to identify stains.

Is it blood or ink?

Kites

It's a windy day. Mix and Max are flying their kite. Kites use the push of the wind to make them fly. How many other things in the picture are moved by the wind?

Mix and Max's kite

This kite is easy to make and guaranteed to fly!

You will need

a large plastic rubbish bag
2 garden canes (or 5mm dowelling) about
 90 cm (3 feet) long
sticky tape
a large ball of string
a ruler

Note to Parents

Making and flying your own kite is more fun than flying a bought one. Kite flying makes children aware of the force of the wind and how it can vary from day to day. Select a safe, open spot, away from overhead power lines.

What to do

1 Open up the rubbish bag and cut out the shape below.

2 Cut out the triangular vent. The shape of the vent is not too important; you can make it a circle or a diamond if you like.

3 Reinforce the sharp corners of the vent with sticky tape.

4 Stick the canes in place with sticky tape.

5 Reinforce the points of the 'ears' with sticky tape. Make small holes through the points and tie a 200 cm (6 foot) piece of string to each hole.

6 Tie the free ends of the string together and tie this onto the ball of string.

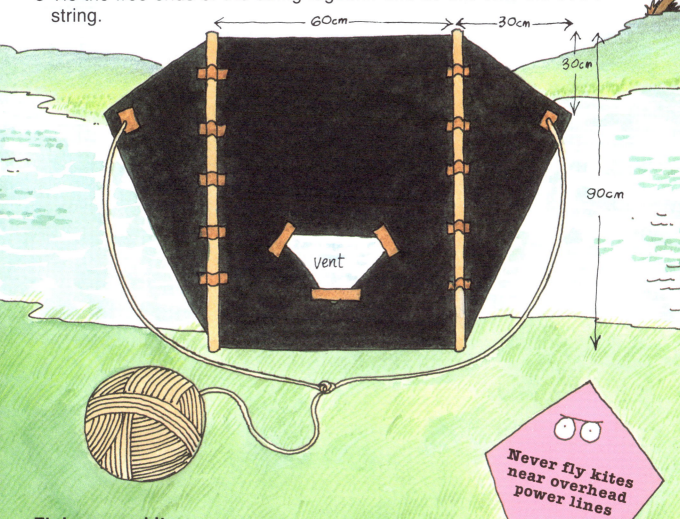

vent

Never fly kites near overhead power lines

Flying your kite

Choose a day when there is a good breeze.

Get a friend to hold the kite. You hold the ball of string.

Walk a few metres away from your friend into the wind.

Call to your friend to let go of the kite and up it should go!

Cartoons

Do you like watching cartoons on TV? This is how you can make your own cartoons.

You will need

A strip of stiff paper or thin card 65 cm by 7 cm or 26 inches by 3 inches (if you don't have a long enough piece, stick two or three strips together) a dark colour is best; scissors, glue, white paper, felt-tipped pens, a ruler, sticky tape.

What to do

1 Draw vertical lines every 5 cm (2 inches) on the paper strip, like this.

2 Put your piece of white paper over the cartoon pictures on the next page, and trace the outline of each picture using a dark coloured pen. You can colour each picture if you like.

3 Cut out each cartoon picture.

4 Stick the pictures in the right order along the bottom edge of the strip. Space them out evenly.

5 In between each picture, cut out a slot about 4 cm long (1½ inches) and ½ cm (¼ inch) wide.

6 Bend your card into a circle with the pictures on the inside.

7 Stick the ends of the card together with sticky tape.

22

To watch your cartoon you will need a record player and a table lamp.

Stand your card circle on the record player. Shine the lamp on to the top of the turntable. Turn on the record player.

Note to Parents
This activity is based on the same scientific principle as film and TV. The illusion of motion is created by showing a series of still images one after the other.

Watch the cartoon through the slots. You can see the action best if you sit well back and the room is dark.

If your record player has two speeds, see what effect a slower or faster speed has on your cartoon.

Can you make your own cartoon characters?

Rubbish!

How much rubbish does your family throw away? To find out you will need 5 plastic bin liners, some sticky labels, kitchen scales.

What to do

Label the 5 bin liners – **paper, plastic, glass, metal, food.** Ask everyone in your family to help. For one day, put everything that anyone throws away into the right bag.

Put the old newspapers, empty boxes and sweet wrappers into the **paper** bag.

Bottles and jars go into the **glass** bag.

Tin cans, drink cans and foil wrappings go in the **metal** bag.

Plastic bags and bottles, cling film and plastic bottle tops go in the **plastic** bag.

Potato peelings, scraps of meat, vegetables and tea bags, go in the **food** bag.

At the end of the day weigh your bags on the scales. Fill in the weights below. Use grams (g) for small amounts and kilograms (kg) for large amounts.

One day's rubbish

g or kg of paper

g or kg of plastic

g or kg of metal

g or kg of glass

g or kg of food

Can you use your calculator to work out how much of each sort of rubbish you throw away in a week?

One week's rubbish

g or kg of paper

g or kg of plastic

g or kg of metal

g or kg of glass

g or kg of food

Note to Parents

Get your child to cross out g or kg as appropriate. Discuss whether it is 'fair' to extend one day's findings to a whole week. It might not be a typical day. It would be more accurate (but less hygienic) to collect several days' rubbish. You could calculate a month's rubbish and a year's rubbish.

Which items could be recycled?

Look Max. It's not all rubbish.

These glass bottles and jars can be used again to make new glass.

We can mend the bat…

and these newspapers can be used again to make more paper.

Timing

Mix and Max are timing things in seconds.

How long does it take to drink a glass of water?

It takes 6 seconds to walk up the stairs.

Max has a digital watch which looks like this.

These two numbers are the seconds. You can watch them count to 60 and then start again.

Mix has a watch with a second hand like this.

This is the second hand. You can see it move. It takes 60 seconds to go round once.

Mix starts timing herself drinking when her watch looks like this.

When she has finished drinking her water, her watch looks like this.

How many seconds have passed?

Practise timing things in seconds and fill in the boxes.

How long does it take you to drink a glass of water? [ ] seconds.

How long to write your name? [ ] seconds.

26

You can make a water clock to time in seconds.

You will need

a small cardboard box
a plastic lemonade bottle with a screw lid
a bowl
a watch which times in seconds
scissors
paper
sticky tape

Note to Parents

Make a hole in the bottom of the bottle with a skewer. If the plastic is tough try heating the skewer in a gas flame.

What to do

1 Ask a grown up to help you make a hole in the bottom of the bottle.

2 Cut a hole in one end of the cardboard box.

3 Stand the bowl in the box under the hole like this. Stick a strip of paper to the bottle. Mark a **zero** line near the top of the strip.

4 Put your finger over the hole in the bottle. Fill it up with water to the zero line. Screw on the top. Put the bottle on top of the box over the hole.

5 Make sure you can see your watch. Start the water clock by taking the lid off the bottle. Every 10 seconds, mark the water level on the paper strip. If you want to stop the clock, screw the lid back on. When the bottle is empty, write the numbers of seconds on the marks you made on your paper strip.

6 Now you have a clock you can use for timing things!

Electric circuits

You will need

a battery
a torch bulb in a holder with 2 wires connected
a length of wire
paper clips

Note to Parents
If **carefully** supervised, your child
will find this circuit simple to mak
and very instructive.
Torch bulb holders, bulbs and wire
can be bought from any hardware
store and most toy shops. Your child
will need help to strip the plastic
insulation off the **ends** of the wire. A
4.5V (3R12) battery has metal strip
terminals that are easy to connect
to. Use a 4.5 volt or 6.0 volt bulb.

What to do

Connect one wire to each of the metal strips on the battery.

You can use paper clips to hold the wires in place.

The bulb should light up. This is called an electric circuit. The
electricity from the battery travels along the wires, through the bulb
and back to the battery.

**Important warning 4.5V
batteries are perfectly safe
but children must never
experiment with mains
electricity. The high voltage
of the mains could cause
death by electrocution.**

Take one of the wires off the battery. Connect another wire so that your circuit is like this.

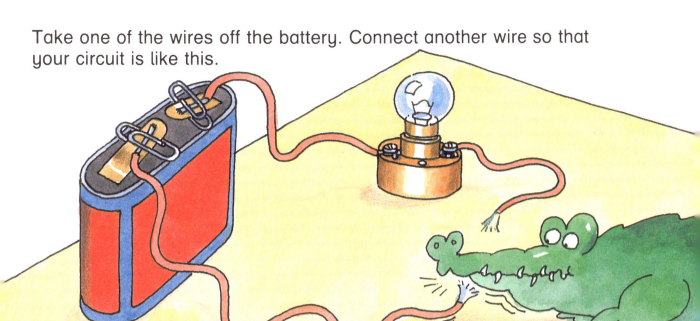

Touch the bare ends of the two wires together. What happens?

Now try touching the wires to either end of a metal spoon. Does the bulb light?

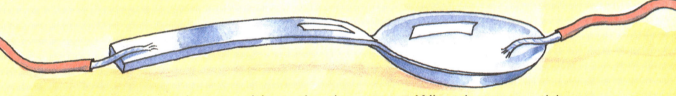

Try the same experiment with a plastic spoon. What happens this time?

Things that let electricity through, like the metal spoon, are called **conductors.** Things that don't let electricity through are called **insulators**.

Use your circuit to test lots of things. Fill in the table and put a tick in the right place.

	conductor	insulator
metal spoon		
plastic spoon		
paper clip		
pencil		

A sundial

A sundial is a clock that uses shadows to tell the time. This is how you can make one.

You will need

a pencil
some modelling clay
a sheet of card
a felt-tipped pen
a watch or clock

a sunny day!

What to do

1 Start first thing in the morning.

2 Choose a place for your sundial. It should be somewhere that is sunny all day. It could be inside by a sunny window or outside in the garden.

3 Lay the card on a flat surface. Stand the pencil so that it casts a shadow on the card. Hold it in place with modelling clay.

4 Look at your watch. When it is exactly – 8 o'clock, 9 o'clock or 10 o'clock mark the pencil's shadow with your pen. Write the number of the hour by the mark.

5 Every hour make another mark. At the end of the day you will have a complete sundial.

Note to Parents
The activity will make children aware of the apparent motion of the sun through the sky. In fact, it is because the Earth is spinning that the shadow moves. The Earth's spinning is also responsible for the day/night cycle.

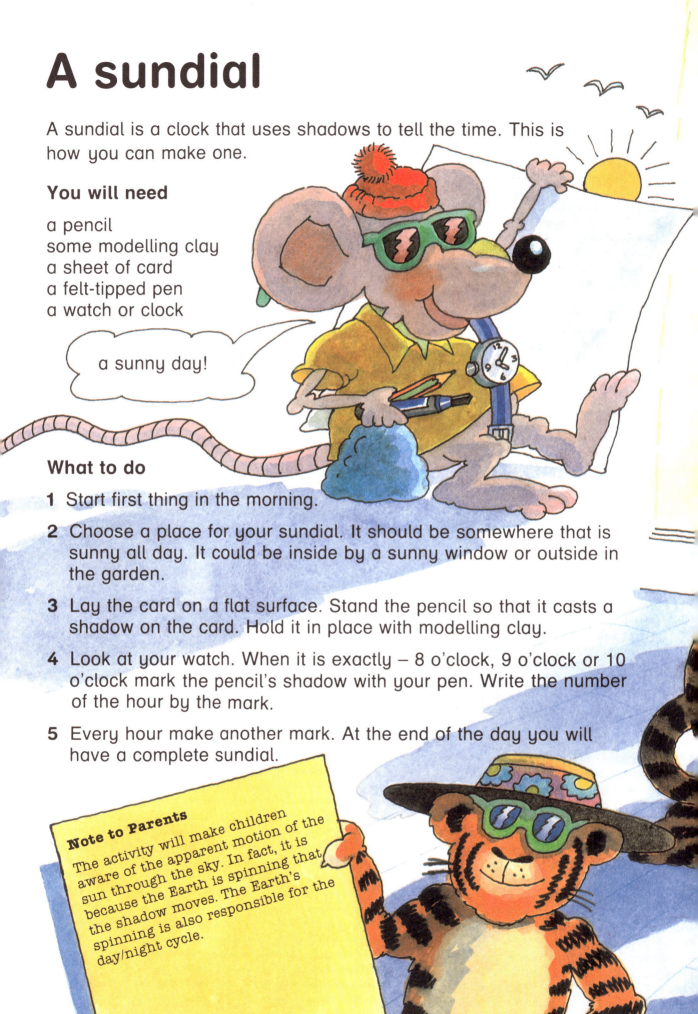

More about the ideas in this book

The emphasis in primary school science today is on the children's own practical investigations. By doing their **own** experiments and making their **own** observations and discoveries children learn far more effectively than they would by reading or listening passively.

The National Curriculum divides children's work in science into separate areas or **attainment targets**. Each target is concerned with a different part of science, and the curriculum sets out detailed programmes of study for each target which your child's teacher will follow in the classroom.

Children's performance in science will be monitored at ages 7, 11, 14 and 16. Their progress will not be measured simply in terms of their knowledge of facts. Their understanding of scientific ideas, and their abilities to plan and carry out scientific investigations, will be equally important. Through investigations such as those in this book, they should develop the skills to plan and predict the outcome of experiments, interpret their observations, draw conclusions and communicate their findings. Taken together the four science books in the Parent and Child Programme provide a complete range of activities to help your child progress in virtually all the target areas. The **Notes to Parents** on the individual activities highlight some of the knowledge and skills which the children will be using as they conduct their investigations.

There are of course close links between science and technology; several of the activities in this book involve children in making something with a practical application – a cotton reel engine to pull a load, a kite that flies and a water clock to measure time. Through making and experimenting with these things, children will start to learn how machines work and what they can and cannot do, as well as developing practical skills of construction and measurement.

Science cannot be learnt in isolation from other areas of the school curriculum. As they work through the material in this book, children will be using and developing both language and number skills. Some words that may be new, such as 'attraction' and 'repulsion' are introduced to describe how things behave. When a new word like this crops up make sure that your child understands what it means in the context in which it is being used. Your child will also be using mathematical skills of measurement, estimation and calculation; encourage your child to use a calculator where appropriate.

Perhaps the most important thing at this early stage in a child's science education is the development of positive attitudes towards enquiry – the desire to have a go and see what happens and the willingness to talk about ideas and discoveries.